ADSIT'S POETRY ANTHOLOGY,
VOLUME I

Thoughts and Inspiration Afield

The Stillness of Nature Speaks Louder Than a Choir of Voices.

TIM L. ADSIT

iUniverse, Inc.
Bloomington

Adsit's Poetry Anthology, Volume I
Thoughts and Inspiration Afield

iUniverse books may be ordered through booksellers or by contacting:

iUniverse
1663 Liberty Drive
Bloomington, IN 47403
www.iuniverse.com
1-800-Authors (1-800-288-4677)

ISBN: 978-1-4502-8815-6 (pbk)
ISBN: 978-1-4502-8817-0 (cloth)
ISBN: 978-1-4502-8816-3 (ebk)

Printed in the United States of America

iUniverse rev. date: 2/2/2011

Dedication

This poetry collection is dedicated to three deceased contributors: Reecie Lillian (Dawson) (Carter) Adsit, my grandmother, and Reverend Glyn Bemister (Carter) Adsit, and Alice Jean (Dowd) Adsit, my parents.

Contents

About the Author and Contributing Poet(s)

Reecie Lillian (Dawson) (Carter) Adsit, Contributing Poet

Reecie L. Adsit was born in Jola, Arkansas in 1895. She married and divorced Roy M. Carter and later married Cyrus Boyd Adsit who died in a plane crash. Widowed, she raised four boys and one girl on a hairdresser's income. She died on March 17, 1974 in El Cajon, California.

Reecie Lillian (Dawson) (Carter) Adsit holding the author

Reverend Glyn B. (Carter) Adsit, Contributing Poet

Glyn B. Adsit was born July 6, 1917 in Catoosa, Oklahoma. He was best known as a teacher, missionary to Hofei, China, minister, and outdoorsman. He and his wife Jean had two children, Jan and Tim. He died March 20, 1999 in Brookings, Oregon. He loved to write poetry.

Reverend Alice Jean (Dowd) Adsit, Contributing Poet

Jean Adsit was born April 3, 1919 in Marysville, Missouri. She was best known as a missionary to Hofei, China, minister, and teacher. Jean and her husband Glyn served together as pastors for 44 years. She loved to read and write poetry. She died on May 5, 2000 in Brookings, Oregon.

Reverend Glyn B. and Alice Jean Adsit

Tim L. Adsit, Author

Tim Adsit was born to missionary parents in Hofei, China on April 26, 1948. He is best known as a successful teacher, school administrator, author, business owner, pastor, and outdoorsman. He possesses a Doctor of Divinity and advanced degrees in education and administration. He is married and lives in Bend, Oregon.

Tim L. Adsit, Author

Foreword

"The Stillness of Nature Speaks Louder Than a Choir of Voices"— Adsit's Poetry Anthology, Volume I—Thoughts and Inspiration Afield by Tim L. Adsit, his grandmother and his parents is a book of inspired and inspiring poetry that the reader will enjoy for a very long time and will want to return to often and reflect upon. Each of the poems is a delight in itself and an opportunity to reflect upon human and natural worlds of which we are all a part. The companion photos beautifully capture the mood and reflection of the poems.

From his cozy cabin in Bend, Oregon and out of his large store of knowledge and experience in the outdoors gained from camping, hiking, hunting, and fishing for over 50 years, Dr. Adsit makes practical observations on human life and on the life of nature. Those who have read his other books know that his powers of observation are keen and considerable, and that his gift for making natural objects and animals humanly interesting and important is indeed remarkable. He writes in a warm, personal, sometimes humorous, rarely forced and effortless style that nicely conveys his reflections and ponderous mood.

As you read the thoughts and meditations of Dr. Adsit's grandmother, tried by the fire raising five children alone during the depression, and his parents, missionaries to China and more than half a century as church leaders, you will clearly see where Tim gets his ability to tap into life-flow of men, nature and God Himself, and allows us to drink deeply from his potent insights.

"The Stillness of Nature Speaks Louder Than a Choir of Voices"—Thoughts and Inspiration Afield will make an excellent gift book, a poetry collection that one will want to have not only on his reading table or shelf but also on that of a friend. The keenness of these observations and the warmth of the author's enjoyment of the out-of-doors world are infectious, passionate and alone rewarding, but each of the poems also arrives at human meanings and understandings. The book is written quietly and unpretentiously and is a lovely book of poetry. The volume may become a favorite with many of

those who love all of God's creation. Edifying, and good, and freshly put, this excellent book deserves a wide reading and thoughtful meditation. The collection is a rare treasure with other volumes sure to follow.

Rev. Christopher B. Adsit
September 29, 2010

Reverend Chris B. Adsit is Co-Founder of Military Ministries, a leader in Campus Crusade for Christ's Personal Disciple making Ministry, a bestselling author, former championship level decathlete, and avid outdoor enthusiast. He and his wife, Rahnella, live in Eugene, Oregon.

Preface

I feel very fortunate to come from a poetry heritage and legacy that has deep roots in my family tree. What makes this book really special is the resonance of three generations of poets, combined into one collection. I have clearly sought to honor my parents and grandmother, as well as the poetic lineage and themes they all share.

In addition, on my mother's side of the family, one of her sisters, my aunt, Gladys Burns had a son named Ralph. Dr.Ralph Burns is considered by many to be a "world class" American Poet.

Ralph Burns was born in Norman, Oklahoma, in 1949, and received an MFA from the University of Montana. Dr. Burns is currently a professor of English and co-director of creative writing at the University of Arkansas at Little Rock, where he has taught various graduate and undergraduate courses including poetry writing, online poetry writing, introductory creative writing, form and theory of poetry, living writers, and the modernist and contemporary long poem. He has also directed a number of honors theses. Burns has frequently taught at summer writer's conferences, such as the Indiana University Writers' Conference. From 1985 to 2001, he also edited the literary journal, *Crazyhorse*. His most recent book, *Ghost Notes*, winner of the FIELD Poetry Prize, was published in 2000 by Oberlin College Press. Burns' five other books include: *Swamp Candles*, winner of the Iowa Poetry Prize (University of Iowa Press, 1996); *Mozart's Starling* (Ohio Review Books, 1990); *Any Given Day* (The University of Alabama Press, 1985); *Windy Tuesday Nights*, winner of the Mountains of Minnesota Award (Milkweed Editions, 1984); and *Us*, winner of the Great Lakes Colleges Association New Writers Award (Cleveland State University Press, 1983). Burns has published over 200 poems in journals, such as *The Atlantic, Poetry, The Kenyon Review, Shenandoah, The Southern Review,* and *Field*. He has also received two National Endowment for the Arts Fellowships in Poetry, the Porter Prize for Literary Excellence, and the Faculty Excellence Award in Scholarship at University of Arkansas at Little Rock, and a Poetry Fellowship from the Arkansas Arts Council.

Thus, poetry has always been in my blood, heart, and soul. By reading the reflections, thoughts, meditations, and themes found in the poems in this collection, you will immediately come into the wonderful world of nature and human nature. In a very straight forward, informal, and warmly personal manner, I have tried to disclose the marvelous and secret world of nature that provides insight into what and who we are, what attitudes I believe that we should take toward life and its Creator, and the way in which we should grow in knowledge and humility.

Many themes are focused upon in these poems such as: Love, children, family, home, birth, life, death, faith, spirituality, God, nature and human nature, friendship, outdoor inspiration the seasons, wilderness, pets, humor, retirement, America, patriotism, hunting, fishing, hiking, camping, perseverance, risk-taking, goal attainment, and reflections from a log cabin.

As the subtitle indicates, these thoughts and inspirations afield are not limited to one particular season only. They have all been discussed here through the written word, and lead the reader into joyful and restful meditation through the seasons.

It is my fervent hope that you find the volume mind-challenging and soul-enriching.

Sincerely,

Tim L. Adsit

Acknowledgments

Some of my poems have appeared in the following publications, to which grateful acknowledgement is made.

The National High School Poetry Anthology, 1964: "My Thoughts Are On the Great Northwest"

A Collection, Harrisburg Union High School Literary Magazine, April 13, 1981, 2nd Edition: "These I Have Loved, No. 1"

Mustang Review: "On Freedom's Wing"; "The Spike and the Royal Bull"

Thanks to my wife, Maggie, who has listened to more elk, deer, cougar, bear, chukar, quail, pheasant, mountain grouse and fish stories, and tolerated more hunting and fishing seasons and time afield away from home, than any one woman should ever be expected to put up with in any marriage relationship. However, if the truth were known, she enjoyed the time catching up on her shopping, visiting with friends and not having to perform her usual domestic responsibilities.

Introduction

An anthology is a collection of selected writings and in this case, the writings selected are a group of original American poems and free verse written by Reecie L. Adsit, Reverend Glyn and Jean Adsit, and Tim L. Adsit representing three generations of poets from one family linage.

The anthology is organized by separate contributing poet and where possible, by themes within each poet's collection. Rather than mixing all the poems together and presenting them under different themes running throughout the entire volume, the author purposely wished to honor and feature each poet's contributions separately and because of this, some of the early poems by the author's grandmother and parents don't focus as much on nature themes as the collection of poems by the author.

With these inspiring thoughts and poetic images, the author and contributors bring us immediately into the beautiful world of nature and human nature. In a very relaxed and warmly intimate and sometimes humorous manner, they reveal the special and inspiring world of nature that provides insight into what we are as human beings, what attitudes and beliefs we should take toward life, its Creator, death, and faith, and the way in which we should mature and develop daily in wisdom, knowledge, understanding, and humility.

Tim usually gets his inspiration for writing and composing poetry when he is hunting, fishing, camping or walking in the great outdoors, and he is well known for carrying a notepad or 3 by 5 cards and a small pencil or pen with him wherever he goes so he can write down his thoughts while being inspired "afield," and then return to his office setting to further refine his thoughts, reflections, and poems.

Tim Adsit is quick to notice even the smallest details while he travels afield, and in his own way, he points out their exquisite beauty in his poetry and prose. Even the smallest things do not escape Tim's experienced eye; and almost imperceptibly he passes from the subject of his poem to bring his new discoveries and insights to our attention.

Glyn, Jean, Reecie and Tim at once see connections between the creatures and situations in the fields and woods, in ponds, streams, and lakes, and the various situations, challenges, and opportunities in our own lives. Transforming their often inspiring thoughts into pleasing rhymes, free verse, and sentences, they endeavor never to become too "preachy," or resort to flat, dull, or trite remarks. They are uniformly at home in both nature and grace, and they speak of both with experience, authority, and enthusiasm. There is an abundance of fresh, creative, often humorous material here and Glyn, Jean, Reecie and Tim have a genuine gift for discovering and presenting new ideas in refreshing ways showing that *"there is a stillness in nature that speaks louder than a choir of voices."*

POEMS BY REECIE LILLIAN (DAWSON) (CARTER) ADSIT

Themes of Love, Children, Family, Home

THE VANISHED YEARS

Where have they gone the darling years;
Of baby mirth and baby tears?
What happened to the hours spent,
With toys and books in deep content?

And whither went the spells of mumps?
Of measles, chicken-pox, and bumps?
Those later years, where have they fled,
Of bats and balls and knees that bled?

Dear God, I was so hurried then.
Could I but have my babies again;
How eagerly I'd join the fun,
And leave a task or two undone.

Could I call back those years today,
I'd be so tranquil, sweet and gay.
Please let them, O God, remember me,
Not as I was, but meant to be.

(Reprinted with permission from Adsit, Reverend Glyn B., "Things On My Mind," The Church Life Bulletin, First Christian Church, Orange, California, Volume XVII, Number 24, Friday, May 6, 1955)

LITTLE BOYS

Father, I've loved the little boys you gave unto me.
When they were very small I loved their star like baby hands,
Their rose bud mouths, dimpled knees and crumpled toes,
Their tousled heads and turned up nose.

I tried to protect them from splinters in their feet,
I prepared foods especially for them to eat,
I crumbled up inside at the thought of any pain for them,
When I heard their cries,
My joy was complete when thru my efforts,
I brought looks of contentment to their eyes.

When school age was reached,
I saw them march away,
Small backs straight, heads held high
Sturdy legs carrying them, arms swinging bravely
As they joined playmates passing by.

I loved their little manliness, the masculinity of their stride
The bravery they professed and didn't feel
Until at evening time I held them close by my side.
And wondered if the teachers noticed their very special appeal.

I tried to protect them from all harm such as children encounter
As they live in childhood and grow.
Such eternal anxiety only a mother's heart can know,
As they grew from childhood into men

And went their separate ways
I felt I'd won over the world of care and could relax
And wait for quieter days.

I love them now for the stand they took on important issues
That they faced from day to day,
I loved them for being determined to win,
Yet, using wisdom and judgment
All along the way.

Now I long to protect them from temptation
And the common enemy, ill health,
And to see them stand firm and true,
Not to waiver while in the search for wealth.
I could not bear to see them suffer day by day
Neither from sickness or sin,
A mother doesn't forget they were little boys
Because now they are men.

Do Babies Laugh in Berlin?

Bombs are falling!

Frantic voices calling,

Then a hush, deadly quiet creeps in,

Mothers clasp babies to breast,

Mothers faint, weary from lack of food and rest.

But do babies smile sweetly, demure?

Do mother's arms feel secure?

Do babies laugh in Berlin?

What mother has not known

Release from burdens that have flown

When baby's smiles begin?

Do war mothers have this blessing still?

God grant it so, if it be they will,

Let babies laugh again in Berlin.

WHITE CANDLES ON A BIRTHDAY CAKE

Little white candles on a birthday cake

Placed there with love and artistic care,

By a young dark eyed mother so young and fair.

Only sixteen candles, though I'm three times sixteen and more,

I shall treasure the unspoken tenderness

The touch of beauty there,

The token of youth and happiness

Will walk with me into distant days

To lighten my burdens and cares.

My Grandchildren

As I watched my grandchildren fair
Swinging on a high hill, wind in their hair,
Uplifted faces filled with glee,
Bringing visions of my own little ones back to me.

Father guide them as they grow,
Watch carefully as they upward climb,
Make Thy presence felt,
So that they may know
Their innermost thoughts are also Thine.

I'M NOT LONELY

I've heard them say,
"She lives alone, her life was so busy,
Now, does she stay"?
The place is so lonely, so still,
She does her little chores, nothing more,
Day by day.

Little do they know as I sit or move
About the place,
I do not see empty stillness,
But four little boys and a little girl
With smiling face.

They stand upon the mound at the end of the garden
While March wind blows in their hair
To greet the first morning of Spring
With gleeful laughter and joyous play, as they scamper there.

They run on eager feet to see a yellow blossom of the Jonquil,
The first to appear
They pause breathless at the beauty,
Never a thought of worry or care.
They chase the Robins just to see them fly,
They pester me for pennies, a kite to buy.
It's Summer, they swim in the pool,
They clamor for food and cool refreshing drink,
Nestling down on shady porches,
Filled with childish pleasures, too tired to think.

The old piano seems to boom with noisy practice,
As a kitten gives up its place upon the keys,
A shepherd dog lies across the doorway,
They step over him, he sleeps on, at ease.

The Autumn brings eager school days,
They march away for a little while
At evening they return, their mind filled with stories,
That only school days can bring
Into the life of a little child.

Then comes the Winter season,
Their muddy boots and rubbers by the door,
The joyous Christmas we share together,
Then looking for Spring, once more.

I'm not lonely, I've earned this place of quiet rest,
This house filled with memories,
Each shining pleasure with the love of God is blest,
A home filled with happy memories where young men
And their wives, and a young women with husband true,
Come often to sit and visit,
They bring their little ones too,
I'm tired when they go, but happiness I've found,
It's hard to remember, was it their little ones or mine
That played upon the garden mound?

A Desire to Touch His Hand

In praying, it seems He is so far away.
I long to know Him, to hear Him say,
I'm here, my child, be still.
Know that I am God, obey My will.

I go my way,
Throughout the day,
Unsatisfied, wishing still
That somehow it would be revealed to me.
Now, with mortal eyes I might see
The Master who has so kindly fashioned me,
Then I could show I love the Lord.
I should greet Him with a look of sweet accord,
I should clasp His hand in mine,
Walk with Him, talk with Him,
And ask Him to my house to dine.

Oh, happy hours to me are given,
The veil is torn asunder,
I've known a glimpse of Heaven,
I now know the touch of His dear hand,
I cried aloud, He heard my plea
And in a gentle way revealed Himself to me.

A neighbor cried in pain, I soothed her feverish brow,
I comforted a little child who had lost in a game of play,

I spoke kindly to one whose color is not of mine,
Feeling skin and enjoying a friendship as we walked along the way.

I visited lonely old folk,
Gathered wisdom of their years,
I whispered hope to many
To still their trembling fears.
My days are filled with service
Toward my fellowman,
sweet peace, I have felt
The Master reach out and touch my hand.

Themes of Nature and Human Nature

THE GIFT OF PEACE

Stand beneath a tree in Summer,
Let city's noises hush,
Listen intently
To the song of thrush.

Gaze through trembling leaves to Heaven,
Let stars look into your eyes,
Grow closely related to the green earth
And to the skies.

When the silver plow of dawn
Cleaves the somber dark,
You will find the gift of peace
Has nestled in your heart.

LOOK AWAY

When things are troubling you, look away!
Pick out a spot you can see from your window or door
Or perhaps a mental picture you may have in store,
See a small white cloud scurrying across the sky
Like tiny baby dresses, hung on a line to dry.
 Though your troubles may be as bothersome as a dead limb
  Of a tree, scraping against an empty house,
  Don't let it fret you my darling as you try to think things out.
  There's a clump of purple violets in a shady nook,
  Let your mind wander a little farther and see a babbling brook.
Distance lends enchantment
Memory will lend you wings
Visit places you'd forgotten
Recall the thrill of little things.
 See small ants carrying their babies from ant hills
  Out into the sunshine of Spring,
  Why, you can rest from all your worries
  Just by watching little things.
Look at snowy cherry blossoms
Banked against a sky of blue,
Look away, far away, my darling
When things are troubling you.

CLOVER BLOSSOMS ON A DRESSER SCARF

Clover blossoms, blooming so sturdy and fair,

Red and white, speaking as staunchly as the stripes

On the flag we love so dear,

Embroidered by loving hands, a young mother's hands,

Guided thru busy hours,

That can turn from artistic things to soothe a feverish brow,

Or comfort a child in pain,

These clover blossoms strengthen me,

They whisper of green meadow grass and sparkling rain,

And things of long ago.

They encourage me to keep onward, to stand staunch,

To rise again should I fall beneath a blow.

Poems and Free Verse by Glyn Bemister (Carter) Adsit

Recurring Themes of Love, Family, Children,
Life, Death, Faith, Nature, Friendship

I Loved You

My life has had its ups and downs,
Sometimes good and sometimes bad,
Sometimes happy, sometimes sad,
But through it all, I loved you.

I smiled when each of you were born,
In my own way I loved you.
I could not know—what the years would bring,
Whether together we would be, or apart.

You grew in your own ways, and watching—I took pride;
Though not always was I able to be at your side.
And now, through eyes made clear by death—God has granted me to see—
that through it all
I loved you, and you loved me.

I Like Men Who Fish

I like men who fish! Men who seek the challenge and the comfort of the ocean, the river, the stream, the lake, the sea.

Men—who laughing say, "When my time comes to go, let it be the fish on one end, on the other end me." Let it be like that dear Lord, when the final call comes.

Let me be there—on some stream, with loved ones or friends…happy, hoping for a strike, or a nibble, or a bite…let me be showing my faith… that I will catch one before the day is gone…there—call me home… suddenly—free me from physical limitations.

And when I arrive in my heavenly home…just one request dear Lord, for all who have gone before me…those good friends of mine who love to fish…let them be there to welcome me…And Lord, give me a job, make me keeper of the streams, the rivers, the lakes…for that will be Heaven to me.

*I Like Men Who Fish, Photo taken by Tim L. Adsit showing
Rev. Glyn B. Adsit holding up fish on a stringer we caught
at East Lake, Oregon in 1991 © TLAW, Inc.*

GOD HAVE YOU ADDED IT UP?

God, have you added up this score of my strivings and my failings? Have you taken into account my heartbreaks, my tears—when I have sought to be better than I am, but failed? I've had my share of hates and loves. I have been searching for myself. I found such joy in fixing things...tinkering they call it. Dear God fix me now.

Some Will Say I Do Not Believe in God But, Let Me Tell You Something ...

What are you? A Dahlia bulb ... you say. Can life or beauty come from that ugly shriveled up seemingly lifeless thing? How can I know if life will come?

Do I dare venture ... have faith enough to trust? Can I have faith to wait after the bulb is planted out-of-sight into the ground? Why should I believe that life will come?

"Try me", please, cries the Dahlia ... "try me and see".

And so I tried ... I who was born and lived all my life in this incredibly beautiful valley ... I risked my faith on a ugly bulb ...it took faith I tell you to believe that anything could come from it at all.

Oh, blessed God: what beauty bursts in my garden. Colors like rainbows.

What shall I do with this beauty? Keep it for myself. I cannot—I give it to my fellowmen that they may learn also to have faith enough to plant and pray and wait. And so my beauty spreads from garden to garden—until my faith grows stronger as their faith in waiting for life to come—is proved. He who plants an ugly bulb—believes in God. He has seen what God sends—beauty for ashes ...

And thus, it is that I am not afraid to die. I am like those Dahlia bulbs. Some will doubt that I can survive to produce life ... but I rest my case ... I put my life in the soil of God ... I wait for the life-giving blood to quicken me ... and I will blossom before God ... and I shall cry out, "have faith, life does come from what is planted in the ground".

I Was Your Teacher

I was your teacher. I taught you to read, to write, to add and subtract. But more—I poured myself into your lives—I sought to inspire, to guide, to insist that you do the best that you could do. I had no children of my own. But, you are my children as surely as if I had given you birth. For a while, I had you in my keeping even more than your own flesh and blood mothers. I helped you put on your snow shoes and I dried your tears. I listened to your heartaches and joys. Yes, when small, I mothered you. And then you grew up and left. But still I went with you in your dreams, your plans, and your accomplishments.

After a while, other small ones came to me and as I looked at them, I saw you again … yes, they were your children. How happy I was to see you in them … and to know that my teaching you had been successful …That you had made it through marriage and child-bearing, and that you had returned to me in your children. The process started all over again … reading, writing, and arithmetic …heartaches and joys, Fall, Winter, Spring, and Summer. And then after 50 years of teaching came my time to step out and let younger ones come into the school and carry on.

I have followed you all these years of my retirement. I have lived in you. Now, that I am what men call dead, you must live for me. So much needs to be done. I ask that you do it. Go on out into life and read and write and help your fellowmen. I never gave you these priceless treasurers to be selfish with them. They will only help you as you use them for God and your fellowman.

I want you to know that I have been given a job to do up here in God's heaven. I watch the little ones—those whose lives were cut short on earth … those who never grew up to adulthood. I gather them around me and we love each other and all of you. And every time the bell rings to signal the entrance of another life into our midst, I hasten to the gateway to see if it is one of my children that I had taught on earth.

Do you remember how timid you were that first day you came into my school room on earth, how fearful you were? It might be like that when you come up here to heaven. I want you to know that I will be here, just like I was there, to greet you and to help you learn the things you will need to know to make it up here in heaven. Things like learning how to brush and trim the Angel's wings ... how to mix the colors that go into the rainbows shining all over the earth ... Don't be afraid of death ... I made it through and the joy I know has helped me to forget the pain and suffering of earth. I must go now ... I hear the bell ringing—someone else is coming ... perhaps it will be you.

GRANDPA'S GONE

Grandpa's gone they say. Yes he died the other day—but still he lives.

He lives in sons and daughters, and even more in grandkids galore.

He lives in friends, who will remember. He lives in memory that shall never fade away.

And very much he lives in love of wife who shared his life in meaningful ways.

It's true grandpa's gone—but he's still here in things he did and said.

He's in your hearts and minds and thoughts and will be there forever.

To loved ones he might say—"don't be afraid to die—perhaps someday we'll meet again

Where God is—beyond the sky."

We'll accept that, and believe it too.

For love never dies and God is love. Yes, we'll find Grandpa again where he and God are waiting beyond the skies.

God Make Me Worthy of My Friends

My greatest joy on earth shall be
To find at the turning of every road,
The strong hand of a comrade kind,
To help me onward with my load.

But since I have no gold to give,
And only love can make amends,
My daily prayer in life shall be,
"God make me worthy of my friends."

To Crystal—With Love

I loved you little Crystal with the shining eyes.

You were my life, you were and are everything to me.

I did not mean to leave you, but the sea took me and I had to go.

And now you live on earth without me, but not without my love.

Your mother that I loved, loves you still—And always will.

And others like Grandpa and Grandma, will always be there, as will Richard, Monte, Sally and Donna, Aunts and Uncles who care.

Remember me with love. And at night when you say your prayers,

Remember that I will be praying for you, for prayer is a two-way street for those who love.

I will be proud of you as you go to school next year, and all the years after that.

I will know when you get your first kiss from that special young man.

I will know when you get married and have that family of your own.

Yes, I will know and care, for in the realest way, I will be there in your blood, in your genes, in your memories and in your heart.

And so, I wait for you, until your long life is through, for time up here does not matter.

And when you come home to God, as we all must, I will be waiting and will call your name, Crystal,

And you will shout, "Daddy it is you", and the circle of love will be complete,

Me and little Crystal with the shining eyes.

POEMS AND FREE VERSE BY ALICE JEAN (DOWD) ADSIT

Recurring Themes of Faith, Spirituality, Death,
Life, Love, Children, Friendship, and Nature

Tried by Fire

God loved you much to trust so great a grief to you.
He was quite certain of you. Oh, my dear, He knew.
How silver bright your fire tried spirit would come through.
He stood above you, watching, waiting there,
To shield you from a hurt too great to bear.

And he who waited by the furnace saw you rise,
From agony to move above with still, calm eyes.
To go your tranquil way more beautiful, more wise,
The silver of your spirit shining through—
God knew that He could trust this grief to you.

"WHAT CHRIST SAID"

I said, "Let me walk in the fields."
    He said, "No, walk in the town."
I said, "There are no flowers there."
    He said, "No flowers, but a crown."

I said, "But the skies are black;
    There is nothing but noise and din."
And He wept as He sent me back;
    There is more, He said; "there is sin."

I said, "But the air is thick,
    And fogs are veiling the sun."
He answered, "Yet souls are sick,
    And souls in the dark undone."

I said, "I shall miss the light,
    And friends will miss me, they say."
He answered, "Choose tonight,
    If I am to miss you, or they."

I pleaded for time to be given.
    He said, "Is it hard to decide?
It will not seem hard in Heaven,
    To have followed the steps of your guide."

I cast one look at the fields,
    Then set my face to the town:
He said, "My child, do you yield?

Will you leave the flowers for the crown?"

Then into His hand went mine,
    And into my heart came He;
And I walk in a light divine,
    The path I had feared to see.

ON DEATH

It is the loneliness of death
That makes the human heart cry out
Why? Oh, Why?

And yet, we know there is no death.

For long ago our Lord arose—
Victorious over death and tomb;
Made straight the way,

For us to follow, ere our fleeting breath.

Thus, sooth our lonely heart and soul,
And fill our empty day with hope forevermore.
Lift up your eyes unto the Lord—Victorious!
Faith is not gone, tis with us still,
Filling our very lives each day.
Tis the beginning, not the end of life,
Sing Praises—glorious.

THOUGHTS ABOUT PAT

They told me he was dead.

Those eyes that loved the trees and mountains high were closed.

I found it hard to understand or accept, we'd talked of him so often together, you and I Lord.

But that's what they said,

Those eyes that loved to look upon the beauty of your world, were closed.

The smile, the smile still there untwisted from the pain he bore,

An undying faith to find the cure.

But I cried no! He is not dead.

He lives eternally—He left our love and care,

But You were there and so was Alvin to receive him and care for him eternally—

You told us there would be no more pain,

And that lifted some of our hurt and sorrow.

I Love You Just the Way You Are

Now, don't go changing
To please all around you,
Your good look, or what you wear.
Develop your own self, dress to your liking,
Even how you wear your hair.

Grow in wisdom, and in spirit,
Stretch your body and your mind.
Do some fun things, just for nothing,
We love you as you are, just fine!

Do drive careful and be cautious,
Eat the right food, don't ever change.
Sleep late mornings, on your day off—
Be true to yourself and your lively bounce you'll regain.

This poem is written just for you dear
And how I love you from head to toe,
I know you must live life your way—
And I trust your judgment, as you grow.

I know you can't be molded, like clay in a jar.
I think I am understanding, some of your feelings,
And I love you, just the way you are.

FOR TIM

Throughout the day—
At work and play—
I've watched him, Lord.
The patter of his little feet,
His boyish laughter soft and sweet,
I've listened for these, Lord.
His cry for me when things go wrong.
Now, day is done, our home is quiet,
Pray guard and keep him through the night,
I beg of thee, Dear Lord.

It seems like only yesterday,
I held him close to me;
And dried the tears from his eyes.
Then off to school, his books in hand.
If I could find the words to tell you,
The things you taught me <u>every day,</u>
It was all part of Your plan.

BOY OR GIRL

A boy or a girl, who has a choice?
There's something sweet in either voice.
Why, if the Lord were to call me up and say,
Which of the two would you like today?"
I think I'd use one of my broadest grins,
And say, "Send either one if it can be twins."
Why I've heard it said, to some folks discontent,
They took on so, when a boy was sent (for they wanted a girl).
And I've heard tell, others wanted a boy just so,
And when there was a girl, they felt mighty low (for they wanted a boy).

But you know somehow it seems to me,
That every parent should happy be.
That after the Stork he's come and gone,
The good Lord would trust them with either one.
So all we ask that the Lord do,
Is bring mother and child softly through.
Give babe a healthy yell and a shock of hair,
Then boy or girl, and the parents won't care.

Now, I intended to surprise
The parents I selected;
But someone went and put'em wise,
I found I was expected!

But say, I fooled them anyhow,
In spite of all their guesses.

They didn't know for sure tell now,
If I'd wear pants or dresses!

P.S. In case you're interested

I was a _____
My name is _____
I arrived_____
I weigh_____
My parents are_____

My Prayer

To be a little kinder with the passing of each day.

To lighten another's burden, as I trod along life's way.

To share the strength God gave me, to keep me out of sin—

Dear God, please hear my prayer today, I ask thee; Amen.

GRIMM'S FAIRY TALE

Once upon a time, there was a happy love affair.
A boy who said he loved her; a girl who said she cared.
A girl who never doubted she would choose the proper mate;
A boy who was patient when upon her he had to wait.

A boy who never grumbled about the food she cooked,
If the food was much too salty, he would always overlook.
A girl who never grumbled, or made him walk too straight a line,
They lived happy ever after; that is, once upon a time.

Upon His Return

Dear God, my friend came home today,
Be with him on life's short way.
You might not know him by his name,
For his honor, power, or fame.
But you will know him by his smile,
His winning ways, his words worthwhile.
The friends he makes, the ones he keeps,
His cheerful words to all he meets.
He's different from the rest you see,
Dear God this friend belongs to me.

POEMS AND FREE VERSE
BY TIM L. ADSIT

Recurring Themes About Faith, Spirituality, and God

NEARER TO GOD'S BLUE SKY

The oak-tree boughs once touched the grass;
  But every year they grew
A little farther from the ground,
  And nearer toward the blue.
So live that you each year may be,
  While time glides swiftly by,
A little farther from the earth,
  And nearer to the sky.
And enjoy the stillness of nature
  That speaks louder than a choir of voices,
Each day living in God's perfect will,
  Making heavenly over earthly choices.

LISTEN, DO YOU WANT TO HEAR GOD?

In nature there is a silence that speaks;

Long walks are conducive to reflection.

God's universe has a rhythm and definite composition if one listens and seeks,

A silence that resonates and causes contemplation.

It seems the quiet whispers of God are speaking to our soul and spirit in nature at times when we are alone.

If He hasn't been present recently in our lives, as He surely must have been,

He was simply being ignored and shut out while we were at home.

For at home, often days turn to weeks, and weeks into months, still there is no inspiration.

We simply do not enjoy any contemplative moments while being hurried at home or during work activity.

We need to shut out the worries of a busy life by returning to nature, keeping still, enjoying the silence, and hearing God's will and inspiration.

For in nature, one can observe that stillness is always a prerequisite for receptivity.

Listen, do you want to hear God, then go to where there is silence, solitude, and wilderness isolation.

Like telephone and television sets cannot receive messages when they are too filled with static and noise;

People must have stillness first, then later, be tuned in and listening; the order cannot be reversed.

"Be still, and know that I am God," quotes the psalmist with joy.

And our way to be tuned in is by renewing our minds and hearts through prayer and reading Bible chapters and verse.

Even in nature, the wind is often extremely strong and loud, and many people get used to the wind and hardly notice its presence.

So too is the voice of God, it's always present but we fail to give it the correct attention because life itself, like the loud wind sound surrounds and shuts out God's voice.

If we are to listen above the din and noise, we have to calm and quiet our soul, our being, our very essence.

God's voice like the wind has not stopped, it only dropped to a whisper by His choice.

Once we have learned to wean ourselves off the addictiveness of the noise and voices of the world, then perhaps we start to listen.

Listen, do you want to hear God, then find a high, lonesome, quiet place just for you.

For me, it is a special mountain in the Middle Fork of the John Day Wilderness Area, which I have given my own special nickname to and so christened.

For forty years now, I have travelled there to contemplate, commune with nature and God, and silently communicate and have yearly been faithful to making this trek of solitude and renewal.

There, in the stillness of the surrounding nature, I pray, listen, hunt, fish and live for a period of time in silence, not speaking to other humans, except, perhaps. by choice, for a few minutes at the end of the day.

From this experience, I can testify that I have audibly heard and know God, His word, His world, society, and humanity in depth and truthfulness, unfettered by any lies.

The stillness of nature speaks louder than a choir of voices singing in a church on Sunday.

And, I am convinced, we should read the Bible in the anticipation of listening to the voice of God which we should then obey and so live our lives.

FIND YOUR SECRET PLACE

He went up into the hills by Himself to pray.

Jesus knew the experience of a personal dialogue with God whether in the night or day.

When His energy ran low, He found private prayer and meditation to be energizing and strengthening.

What He found, we too can experience if we take seriously our need for private praying.

Jesus planned for His quiet times and He expected results while in His secret place.

Like Him, we must also plan for time apart and expect to sense the personal presence of God and his Grace.

Find your secret place where praying to God is most helpful, remembering to thank Him and asking for forgiveness when you have sinned;

Realizing how God is touching lives today as our personal Savior and friend.

GROWING WITH CHALLENGES

When I look at the soil in my garden after the winter has tempered it,

I am amazed at its softness and readiness to produce growth through the renewed soil and grit.

How different it is from the hard-crusted plot that I saw in the fall.

Yet it is the same soil, only it has been conditioned by the winter and the harshness of it all.

When God looks at my heart, does God see a frozen tundra or a spring garden?

Jesus compared our heart with the soil, is it soft or hardened?

Unlike the soil, we do have a choice to allow the winter of problems and challenges in our life to harden or to soften our heart.

We can choose to be ready for the growth of God's word as we offer ourselves to God to serve and do our part.

So, allow the challenges you meet today to give God the opportunity to condition your heart.

Grow with your challenges and look for the seed of equal or greater benefit in them allowing you and God to make a fresh start.

WE ARE ALL UNIQUELY CREATED

The blizzard raged for twenty-four hours,

Blanketing our meadow around the log cabin with tons of crisp, white snow showers.

I watched the storm, mesmerized by the millions of dancing flakes that filled our visible world.

It was almost impossible to believe that each snowflake is different as it hit the ground, drifted and swirled.

Upon reflection I realized, God is not in the business of mass production,

God is an artist, who paints on the canvas once with no other reproductions.

Just as each person has a unique set of fingerprints, teeth, and DNA code,

A microscope reveals that each snowflake has a unique pattern that the Creator bestowed.

A creation is an extension of an artist and has infinite value, beauty, and worth.

When we are overwhelmed by the blizzards of life, when worries swirl around us like blinding, angry snowflakes, let us take courage—because we are uniquely created and worth so much to God in Heaven and on earth.

Life's Pathway

Dedicated to Toni

I knew the trail was there—somewhere ahead, just out of sight!
The map had shown it so clearly, but it seemed hidden without light.

So I pushed on, exploring the edges of the forest meadow, seeking an opening in the trees.
The wild berry vines and Rhododendron bushes were grown up and seemed to close every possible opening not allowing me to walk free.

Then I found it!
Hardly a hint of the trail existed, but my perseverance paid off, I didn't quit.

Soon I was hiking and walking on a narrow, but a well-marked trail.
It is the same in life and in matters of significance, trust in Jesus and you will not fail.

The trail seems covered up, hidden, and at times, continuing seems to no avail.
However, if we accept the reliability of the map of Scripture and preserve, we shall find the trail!

Recurring Themes About Birth, Life, Death
To be read at my own celebration of life ceremony

"SUNRISE, OH SONRISE"

Jesus had a mansion ready,

He Himself prepared it all;

Then, when I was ready for it

He gave the sudden call.

    My thoughts are on the Great Northwest

    Where my friends and loved ones are gathered today.

    But my soul is in Heaven blessed,

    And, I long to tell you, here I will stay.

Those of you gathered in the presence of my earthly death and body need to realize,

That with Jesus, the last word is not death, but life eternally.

The Master's promise of eternal life is like a sunrise,

And the presence of His living light is glorious to see.

    Yes, I've gone to help your Heavenly Father prepare a place for you,

    That where He is, there you may be also.

    So, when your earthly life and mission on earth is through,

    And, you receive your call, your soul will be led to Heaven's sunrise glow.

And then, you in turn, you will be able to say to your friends and family that the "Son" is stronger than the clouds,

And your God within you is more powerful than any repressive mood that temporarily surrounds my passing from you.

Light is stronger than death's dark shrouds;

Therefore, the "Sonrise" will shine again this new "mourning" with a bright hue,

And warmly comfort with its rays against clouds,

Of white and skies of majestic crystal blue.

TO THE ELK CALF AT BIRTH

Green the cheat grass is springing, tiny purple sage buds appear,
Magpies and cow pies dot the meadows, wildflowers are here.
    All the Malheur birds are coming ,see them on the wing;
    You can hear them singing, come and greet the high desert Spring.
Newly born little elk calf, don't be afraid!
Lift your eyes from the meadow's mossy shade.
    Your mother cow calls for you making sounds across the sky;
    May is here waiting, and here, too, am I.
Come, pretty elk calf, winter's away;
Come, for without you May isn't May.
    Down through the sunny forest hooves on the fly;
    Quick, little elk calf, open your eye.

While You Were Out, Life Called

While you were out, Life called ... and asked, what do you know?
I responded, the more I know, the more I know I don't know.

I asked, why are you appalled?
No, Life responded, but do you know:

> "He who knows not, and knows not that he knows not, is a fool ... shun him!
>
> And, he who knows not, and knows that he knows not, is a learner ... teach him!
>
> And, he who knows, and knows not that he knows, is a sleeper ... awaken him!
>
> And, he who knows, and knows that he knows, is a leader ... follow him"!

I responded, no, I didn't know, and I thanked Life for the call,
And began to ponder it all.

Life's Mascots

Dedicated to Amy and Regina, two teachers with a special dream and passion for teaching kids who are beginning their adventure and journey teaching ...

First as a student, then as a teacher, principal, curriculum director, and superintendent, I have spent my life serving America's children in our public schools.

Each school had a mascot, a thing, an animal, or a person thought to bring good luck.

My life's mascots have included Scotties, Reapers, Harvesters, Trojans, Beavers, Giants, Ducks, Cruisers, Eagles, Indians, Cowboys, Pirates, Bears, and Mustangs and they were all pretty cool.

But by far, my favorite mascot of all was the majestic Eagle who rose above the others from the mire and the muck.

Eagles learn to fly to great heights from a very early age, to weather any storm, to achieve their dreams by riding high on freedom's wing, and to soar in a changing world.

Like the children in my classrooms, until Eagles discover their wings, there is no purpose for their lives.

Until they learn how to soar, they will fail to understand the privilege it is to have been born an Eagle as their lives unfurl.

As teachers and parents, one of the greatest gifts we have to offer is to push our children out of the nest while yet young and alive.

Why does the thrill of our children soaring have to begin with the fear of falling from their nest in this world?

It's that push from the nest that is the greatest gift we have to offer and it allows them to soar on high.

The push is our supreme act of love.

And so one by one we push them out of the nest and they learn to fly.

Proving that even Eagles need a push to enable them to soar above.

Children have been my legacy. They leave my care year after year as inspired people, coming to life with a purpose and passion, with the daily desire to grow and contribute.

My students learned that the purpose of life is to be a growing, contributing human being.

They have learned that their rewards in life will be in direct proportion to the contribution they make each day anew.

So as the Eagle soars high on freedom's wing, let our children's vision soar and lead them on to greater heights of achievement, rallying them on as Eagle mascots in life's moments fleeting.

SUNRISE BUTTE

Glassing a hillside on an elk stand near Sunrise Butte,
I began to reflect on life thinking I was quite astute.

Suddenly, a voice spoke softly in my ear,
Saying, my son, do not fear.

Do your best, keep your promises,
Don't be one of those doubting Thomas's.
I do exist for all to see,
Now, bow your head and pray to me.

So quietly, I prayed reverently in words almost mute,
There on that hillside overlooking "Sonrise" Butte.

Family Tree: The Next Generation

Dave Samuelson's painting entitled Family Tree: The Next Generation;
Is the story of a particular bull elk and provides reflection and inspiration.

The dying bull elk stands before the massive ponderosa pine, drinking from the stream.
His head is bowed low under the weight of his hefty rack, and his body is gaunt and lean.

In the season of his life, days are becoming shorter by the forest stream.
In the foreground a calf, young, vibrant, and fresh, curiously inspects the scenery, reflects on his future life and dreams.

Next to the young calf sprouts a sapling ponderosa pine.
The loss of one generation and beginning of another is about the passage of time.

We've only got so many years to experience wild places and things here on earth;
While continuing to pass the torch, our heritage, and our legacy on to the next generation before we die and nurture our young along to a promising life after their birth.

RIVER BATTLE

In the field, on the ground
Sneaking up on the elk herd without a sound.
Checking the wind
And bringing them in.

With the chirps of a cow call.
Two royal bulls appear ready to give their all.
They step into the shallow river but not to swim or paddle,
Instead, what ensues is a river battle.

Antlers locked together and flashing,
Bodies posturing and thrashing.
Water churning, barely missing willow boughs,
The two bulls battling for breeding rights with a harem of cows.

Muscles bulging,
Horns gauging,
Hooves pounding,
Bugles sounding.

Nostrils snorting
And flaring.
Labored breathing,
Bodies heaving.

Like two prize fighters in the ring,
Dancing and punching back and forth struggling.
Locked in mortal combat, in the middle of a stream,

But in reality, not in a dream.

Survival of the fittest
Is what photographer James T. Jones has presented us.
This famous photograph of the River Battle scene has been framed and set
And is available from www.picturepeddler.net.

MISTY MORNING ELK CHALLENGE

Dedicated to Larry Conaway and the students in his health class at Crane Union High School ...

It's early winter at our hunting cabin;

Snow blankets the majestic mountains.

Winter's solitude has set in;

The woods are peaceful and quiet, serenity surrounds.

Natures' evening performance includes the Northern lights;

We're spending a rustic Christmas together curled up by the fire in our log home.

The tree is decorated with elk figurines of various heights;

A lonesome royal bull atop, satellite bulls all around, made of Styrofoam.

The storm has ended and Rocky Mountain Elk have come to drink from the nearby stream;

Causing my friend and I to just gaze out our cabin window and reflect on past and future hunts.

Together mentally in pursuit of our dream;

We have visualized a misty morning royal bull elk with nine points rising from a huge rack in front.

A herd bull, capable of loud bugles and defending against any challenge;

His senses always alert to humans or other bull elk near his herd of cows.

We sneak up, have him in our sights, but decide not to shoot or make a sound;

For at a distance we see another challenging bull stepping out from behind some fir boughs.

In our dream, the morning uncovers frost on the carpet of yellow grass,

Turning it to mist as the sun peeks over the horizon.

Although the rut is coming to an end at last,

The herd bull's spirit is lively and he is keenly aware of the intruder's bugling and soon the fight will be on.

Ready for battle now, he answers the call of the challenging bull approaching.

Exuding vim, vigor and success, the royal bull stands ready to protect his herd, turf and landscape.

The setting for this fall dream is a forest meadow opening,

And for the combatants, there will be only one able to escape.

THIS DAY WE SAILED ON!

Themes About Risk Taking, Perseverance and Reaching Goals

Columbus kept a journal as he sailed over the Atlantic Sea
While onboard the Pinta, the Nina, and the Santa Marie.
During his famous adventure to discover the New World,
On many nights, encouraged, as his continuing voyage unfurled,

He recorded the day's progress on his journal page,
Where, often he penned this simple and determined message.
This day we sailed on! This day we sailed on!
Christopher Columbus sailed on.

He was driven by the hope of riches and discovery,
And the thrill of exploring uncharted territory.
Though few of us go searching for new worlds these days,
Our lives are nevertheless abundant with daily discoveries as we live, learn,
and grow in new ways.

Just like in our life journey and adventures toward our goal,
Our imaginations must be stimulated, curiosity sparked, and drive to discover
allowed to unfold.
Our journey must be fun, interesting, intriguing, and challenging beyond
expectation,
But realizing it's the journey that counts, not the ultimate destination.

A ship is safe when it is in the harbor,
But this is not what ships are for.

The adventure, the challenge and the rewards are for those who take the journey,

So, go ahead, begin your adventure, and discover what's inside and your ability to be set free.

Like Columbus, never give up, but keep on keeping on,

And say at the end of the day, this day we sailed on!

Come along and soar with me, yearn to be free,

And do whatever it takes to fulfill your ultimate destiny leaving a legacy.

Recurring Themes About Nature, Human Nature,
Outdoor Inspirations, The Seasons, and Wilderness

My Thoughts Are On the Great Northwest

My thoughts are on the Great Northwest,
My soul is homeward bound.
I long to view the mountain peaks
And hear the ocean pound.

To fish the old McKenzie—
Roam the valleys green with grass,
To hear the wind go whispering
In the pines along the pass.

Yes, my thoughts are returning homeward
To the land of the setting sun—
Where one day at the end of my life
I'll be buried by and by.

It's Something Inside That Makes You Want to be Outside

Dedicated to Darcy, one of my daughters ...

It's not something I planned.

It just developed over the years.

It doesn't have a name, it's a feeling, a way of life.

I suppose you could call it the outdoor lifestyle.

You know what I am talking about.

It's something inside that makes you want to be outside.

It's what makes you involuntarily look overhead when you hear the honk of geese,

And breathe a little deeper on crisp winter mornings.

It's what makes you remember the good conversation and coffee, and smell of smoke from a long-ago campfire.

It makes you throw "just one more cast" again and again at the end of the day.

It's knowing there is great delight in simple pleasures,

The reflection of dawn over sparkling water, the hide and seek of fisherman and fish.

It makes your heart swell when your pup places that first retrieve in your hand.

It's that pride you felt from calling in your first bull elk.

It pushes you over that next hill, pushes you to get a little farther up the trail, to that

Little known box canyon or lake, that favorite hunting or fishing spot, that place

You've never seen or been before.

After half a century of hunting, fishing, camping, and hiking at every chance I get,

It's still the outdoor life style that I love.

I've learned to pass on the outdoor way of life, to leave a legacy, and to draw in others

With these same values who have at their core, a deep, personal love of the great outdoors.

As Winter Looses It's Icy Grip

As winter loses its icy grip, bull elk shed their antlers as they begin to leave winter range,

And search for green spring meadow and prairie grass.

In April, the beginning of a new rack appears with a look so strange,

And winter snows begin to melt, and frozen streams, rivers and lakes begin to break up at last.

As winter loses its icy grip, ground squirrels emerge from hibernation and soon mate,

"Sage Rat" litters are born by late spring.

They begin digging holes in rancher's fields making them irate,

And as a result, one can often hear the sounds of bullets ring.

As winter loses its icy grip, migrating birds sweep north again, brightening the woods, meadows and prairies with their songs,

For another cycle of nesting and chick rearing.

And Bald and Golden Eagle chicks hatch in throngs,

While red-tailed hawks are just laying their eggs and preparing for chick bearing.

As winter loses its icy grip, bobcats mate, and kittens will be born in early summer.

River otter pups are born and soon join in the fun making a splash.

Grizzly bears emerge from their winter dens and long slumber,

And search for winter-killed carcasses and new spring grasses to break their long winter fast.

As winter loses its icy grip, spring flowers bloom in mild climates where its warm.

Yellow bells, trilliums, glacier lilies and other flowers sprinkle bits of color on the forest floor.

On the prairie, bison calve in April and May, the newborn calves able to walk and follow their mothers within minutes of being born.

And hundreds of wildflowers mingle among the grasses, painting native prairies with blazing color when they bloom once more.

ROAMING THE HIGH COUNTRY

I have visualized my goal in a tapestry upon my home office wall,

Of a forest scene showing a majestic, royal elk.

The seven point bull is depicted in Fall,

Against a backdrop of excellent details, natural colors, and it gives an autumn ilk.

The bull is roaming the high country,

And travelling through a windless mountain meadow full of grass.

The meadow is surrounded by snags, bogs, and green trees,

Showing the meandering bull crossing the high meadow heading for a game trail on a distant mountain pass.

Like the majestic elk pictured on my wall,

I too like to roam the high country both physically and year around in my mind.

Autumn is the time of year I like best of all, when leaves from trees begin to fall,

And my ancient, nomadic, hunting-gathering instincts begin returning, and I can hunt, enjoy life, and unwind.

Roaming the High Country

Where Steeples and Mountain Eagles Meet

In the afternoon sun of Port Angeles, Washington in spring and winter,

There appears a portrait of an old Indian in the peaks of the Olympic Mountains covered with snow and timber.

It is a huge shadow, looking down upon all activities below.

Legend has it that this was a very spiritual place and the Guardian of the Valley—the seasons foretold;

And the time to return to dig roots, catch salmon and oysters, and the time to leave to prepare for winter's chill,

Where many still believe, he watches over the valley still.

A view of historic Port Angeles from the northwest sea shores captures the "steepled" skyline as it meets the majestic peaks of the Olympic Peninsula Mountains.

The rooftops, afternoon shadows and autumn colors of Port Angeles are punctuated by grandiose steeples and cupolas of some of the finest architecture in Washington with Victorian charm and public fountains.

Port Angeles, Washington, where steeples and mountain eagles meet the sea foam;

One can readily feel the peace and tranquility of the city where you can be at home.

WATERTON PARK REMEMBRANCE

Out of nature's gratitude,

There sprang a lovely miracle;

A lake from among the peaks,

Fed from a subterranean creek

And beautiful snowmelt water fall.

Waterton Park, Alberta Canada,

A scene remembered from long ago on a family vacation.

Pictures taken on a boat trip around the lake,

Made even more beautiful by the rainbow

Glistening through the storm clouds and the lightning's thunderous ovation.

Raindrops pelted the glass windows

Of the enclosed boat.

Waves rocked the craft up and down

And from side to side during the storm,

Causing one to wonder if it would stay afloat.

By day's end, on the lake among the peaks with their purple hue;

The sunlight proved stronger than nature's dark rain shrouds.

And warmly the setting sun comforted with its rays against clouds,

Of white and skies reflecting on waters of royal crystal blue.

High Summer Happenings in Elk Country

Dedicated to my elk hunting companions Loren Bebb, Larry Conaway, Chuck Steves, Dave Doman, and Dwane Thompson ...

In mountain habitats, elk are on the move to the high country in search of summer forage.

Wildflowers are at their peak and all in full bloom.

It's berry season, and woods and thickets are full of ripening berries soon to be ready for picking, canning, and storage.

Young eagles, hawks and osprey are testing their wings, taking their first flights and practicing clumsy landings where dangers loom.

Young ducks are beginning to fly and have almost grown to adult size.

Hummingbirds are buzzing nectar-sweet flowers and feeders.

Chipmunks, ground squirrels and tree squirrels are very active, fattening up and storing food for the coming winter's snowy skies.

In dry sagebrush country, sage grouse and chukars move their almost grown broods to springs and streams to find succulent green plants, cheat grass, and seeds.

Grasshoppers suddenly seem to be everywhere in the summer grass, and trout snap up wayward hoppers that plop into streams.

Bats are active at night, feeding on summer insects.

On warm evenings, eastern woods are lit with fireflies flashing their love messages in hopes of finding a mate it seems.

Raccoons spend their nighttime hours foraging for everything from crayfish and snails to insects, birds, and small mammals and fruit it collects.

In summer, elk often choose beds in cools shade under a dense canopy of trees, and they may move to new beds throughout the day as the sun moves.

These woodland beds often have a grassy carpet, and elk choose spots up against a downed tree or a tangle of brush where their outline is broken from the eyes of an enemy where camouflage protects.

On warm days, elk often move to the deepest shade of north slopes or the cool soil of meadows leaving deep prints with their hooves.

These are a few of the high summer happenings you can often observe in elk country.

High Summer Elk Country

High summer and warm days have come again to Central Oregon elk country.

Elk follow habitual trails as they move through their territory.

Elk cows are focused on caring for their young all day.

Calves are busy with activities that strengthen growing bodies and teach them the ways of being an elk through play.

Herds wear paths through fields and woodlands and high along mountain slopes,

And crossing high mountain meadows awash in wildflowers, watery bogs, and songbirds singing beautiful notes.

Thunderstorms hammer summer skies during this spectacular part of the year.

And cumulus clouds build and grow into powerful storm cells, as warm air rises over the High Cascade mountains and encounters cold, moist air in the atmosphere.

After such storms, soft mud and sand reveal the passing of big game.

The edge of streams and ponds is a good place to look for tracks of deer and elk and the direction they are going and from whence they came.

Yes, camping in high summer elk country stirs my soul, raises the hair on the back of my neck, and brings out the primitive hunter in me almost without reason.

You can feel it coming not too long from now—the autumn leaves, the bugling bulls, the fall rifle hunting season.

Autumn Reflections

Autumn has arrived in elk country.

Pristine landscapes and beautiful vistas are all around.

Fall colors have begun to turn the forest ablaze with reds, oranges and golds.

In the distance, one can see eagles riding wind currents along mountain ranges,

Circling over high ridges as they catch lift from rising thermal currents.

Thousands of snow geese move through the skies on their journey from the arctic to wintering areas in southern states.

Brown trout and brook trout fill the mountain streams.

Beavers are building damns.

Bears are wandering widely, foraging day and night for the last of the berries, fruits and bulbs before hibernation.

Ground squirrels are storing food for the winter.

Mountain grouse and quail abound.

A light skiff of snow has fallen signaling the approach of winter.

The breeding season for elk is ending.

Hunters are making camp up the trail, over the next ridge, in mountain saddles protected from the wind.

Outfitter's tents, trailers, horses, and ATV's appear.

Autumn's clear nights are a time to stargaze, tell stories, visit, develop friendships and reflect on the important things in life around an old-time, well used campfire ring.

The long-awaited elk hunt is here.

Latrines are built and meat poles are up and ready.

It's time to take great delight in simple pleasures—the reflection of dawn over sparkling meadow waters,

And for the game of hide-and-seek between hunters and wily, elusive elk to begin.

As Winter Winds Gust Through Elk Country Landscapes

As winter winds gust through elk country, heavy snow builds up, and elk move to low valleys and slopes where they can better dig through the snow to feed on dried grasses and browse on shrubs.

Winter is a good time for biologists to count elk from helicopters or light airplanes since elk can be seen more easily when leaves are off deciduous trees and shrubs, and the elk are feeding and resting out on open slopes.

Black bears and grizzly bears hibernate in their dens, although they sometimes come out on a warm winter day in late January to play with newborn cubs.

The ptarmigan, long-tailed weasel and snowshoe hare are well adapted to winter and all turn white for perfect camouflage against the snowy winter slopes.

The pointed shape of spruce and subalpine fir trees helps them shed heavy snow.

Elk, deer, moose and other animals may die of starvation in winter, but their bodies provide a feast for scavengers like magpies, ravens, eagles and coyotes.

Mice and voles often stay active in winter, tunneling under the snow, and with no heavy winter coats, they depend on snow to insulate them from the cold air when winds blow.

Owls, coyotes and foxes hunt mice by listening for movement under the snow and pouncing from above in places remote.

Martens and long-tailed weasels hunt for prey under the snow.

On mountaintops, winter winds and blizzards prune the trees into stunted, twisted shapes.

Trout and other fish seek out deep pools in rivers and streams, where the water does not freeze and where they can conserve energy out of the river's flow.

And, geese, swans, ducks and bald eagles winter over on large rivers and coastal bays and capes.

These are my reflections on what's happening as winter winds gust through elk country's landscapes.

AURORA BLISS AT TRAIL'S END

Charles Dickens once said, "Nature brings to every time and season some beauties of its own."

One of my favorite times is Winter and Christmas eve and morning spent at my hunting cabin at trail's end.

The Northern lights make for dancing Aurora Bliss at night in my cabin home.

And all is calm and all is bright on Christmas morning when spent with a friend.

After storm's end, the majestic Rocky Mountain Elk, bugle over long distances almost as if they are sending their Christmas wishes.

It reminds me of times spent with my father and mother and the gift of their love,

Which was greater than rivers of gold filled with silver fishes.

May the gift of His love bring you joy this Christmas season and throughout the New Year may you experience God's peace and joy from above.

Eastern Oregon's Outback

For the last five years, I have lived in Eastern Oregon, a place of awesome beauty—from Hells Canyon's wildest rapids to the glimmering peaks of the Wallowas, from the rolling wheat fields of the Columbia River Plateau to the rugged breaks of the Steen's Mountains.

Many of the streams, rivers, and lakes in the region have warm springs for bathing and artesian fountains.

The skies are wide and blue,

And beautiful scenery unfolds around every bend in the road—where adventure awaits you.

Eastern Oregonians are proud of their heritage—Chief Joseph, Lewis and Clark, Oregon trail pioneers, and those who followed to settle the land.

Their traditions and celebrations are rooted in the earth, the water, the wildlife, the climate, geological formations, the wind, and the Creator's hand.

As you roam Oregon's Outback, take your time,

And travel the back roads so beautiful and sublime.

Come hear the stories and relax in our sunshine,

And marvel at the land called Eastern Oregon—travel back in time.

It's wide open for discovery, from the rivers to the mountains.

Land of scenic wonders and geological tours, complete with green springs and small fountains.

My daughter Darcy was so proud of her first Eastern Oregon trout,

Our fishing experiences were terrific, all across the region we limited out.

Whether traveling along established scenic byways, or back country highways,

73

There is no other place, like Eastern Oregon with its star studded nights and clear, crisp days.

And side trips to ghost towns,

> Where you can walk down the deserted street and let your imagination take you to a time when the community was filled with life's sounds.

Stand in front of the old dance hall and listen quietly.

> On the whisper of the wind, is that a honky-tonk piano playing a tune lightly?

"I'll Take You Home Again Kathleen,"

> It's easy to imagine a shy young man, crisp white shirt, red kerchief around his neck, asking the girl with long, curled hair to dance and with him dream.

Tomorrow the ghosts will all return to work the fields,

> And move the sheep and cattle, but tonight they put their dress boots on and dance both slow waltzes and fast two-steps, clogs, squares, rounds, jigs, and reels.

Just wait until you experience Eastern Oregon,

> You can actually hear yourself think once again.

But take your camera because it's truly where the deer and antelope play,

> And where you can see big horned sheep, wild mustang horses, bald eagles, great-horned owls, sage rats, elk, buffalo, and rattle snakes in one day, not four feet away.

Oregon's Outback is where rural is for real.

> The skies are the bluest blue and the air has a refreshing clean smell and feel.

Bring your ATV, four-wheel drive, horse, mule, walking boots, or mountain bike,

> And join us while you explore some more wherever with permission you like.

Having a good time in Eastern Oregon seems to come with the territory.

Experience a western ranch vacation for the entire family.

"Land of Scenic Wonders", "Oregon's Best-Kept Secret", "the Alps of Oregon", and "God's Country," have all been used to describe parts of Northeastern Oregon.

It's a place for a mountain pack trip you will treasure for so long.

A little walking, a little riding, beautiful views of mountains, rivers and valleys.

All kinds of wildlife and fabulous food to make your spirit rally.

Where you can call an outfitter's tent home.

And spend days in the wilderness, going wherever either you by yourself or with a guide wish to roam.

In the afternoon sun of the Baker Valley in spring and winter,

There appears a portrait of an old Indian in the peaks of the Elkhorn Mountains covered with timber.

It is a huge shadow, looking down upon all activities below.

Legend has it that this was a very spiritual place and the Guardian of the Valley—the seasons foretold;

And the time to return to dig roots and the time to leave to prepare for winter's chill,

Where many still believe, he watches over the valley still.

Or, come explore Southeastern Oregon's "Wild Side and Outback", there is no other place like it on earth.

And don't miss Peter French's Round Barn, the Visitor's Center, and Jenkins Historical Museum, the High Desert Scenic Byway, Crater's of the Moon, and East Steens Tour route complete with the Alvord Desert and Dick Jenkins knowledge and mirth.

Harney County, Gateway to the Steens and more, where Oregon's two largest cattle ranches are found on open range.

Sigh at the sound of a breeze through the quaking aspen leaves and view the roaring springs.

The land is big and vast, and so are our appetites.

What could taste better than a scrumptious hamburger and milk shake at the Fields Store and Café towards late afternoon or night.

Fly fishing is usually great at Mann Lake, especially after a short rain.

And you can top off the journey with a late night steak and fries meal at Crane Supply and then take a dip in the Crystal Crane Hot Springs just outside Crane.

Or, travel around the other way and stop at the Steen's Mountain Resort outside French Glen,

See the Kiger Gorge and then head back to the Narrows for a buffalo burger again.

Rich history and real adventure await,

In this part of the state.

Come visit us just once, and you'll want to come back,

To the Eastern Oregon Outback!

THE STILLNESS OF NATURE SPEAKS
LOUDER THAN A CHOIR OF VOICES

The stillness of nature speaks louder than a choir of voices.

Wild rivers, rugged mountain trails, tall, old growth forests—these are the natural habitat places.

Through the years I have found joy and inspiration in the wilderness settings of the mountains of Oregon.

Whether fishing, hunting, horseback riding, climbing mountain trails, rock hunting, writing poetry outdoors, or photographing nature, my Christian faith and walk has been strengthened and renewed again and again.

Through my closeness with nature, I have received a deeper understanding of God as Almighty Creator and of necessity for man to be an appreciative tenant and steward of the earth.

I feel quite deeply the responsibility man must share for tending our earth, and all who love the vastness and beauty of the great outdoors, will find inspiration while afield and draw closer to God, nature, and mankind experiencing renewal and rebirth.

For the stillness of nature speaks louder than a choir of voices.

And while in nature, one can focus his mind, receive inspiration for solving life's challenges and gain perspective in making clear life's decisions and choices.

The Three Sisters Mountains between Bend and Sisters, Oregon. There is a Stillness in Nature That Speaks Louder Than a Choir of Voices.

Recurring Themes About Love, Family, Home, Children, Parents, Grandparents, Friendships, Pets and Humor

THESE I HAVE LOVED, NO. 1

… . These I have loved;

The shining sun on sparkling lakes,

The graceful ripple an interrupting stone makes;

The sky of blue and grass of green,

The Pacific coastline I have often seen;

The steady rhythm of a crisp parade,

Or the jazzy tempos by a trumpet made;

The sight of home when I've been away,

That makes me never want to stray;

The reassuring bark of my dog in the yard,

And a difficult test that makes me think hard;

And the breaking dawn that introduces light;

The accomplishment of a task well done,

The clear warm radiance of the sun;

My children's laugh and my wife's warm smile;

My mother and father's nurturing and counsel in life all the while.

All these have been my loves …

MOTHER'S SEEDS

Dedicated to mom as a eulogy at her celebration of life service.

Like the ripples on a quiet lake, set free,

That are caused by skipping stones and rocks,

A teacher affects eternity;

She can never tell where her influence stops.

Mother was such a teacher and friend,

She planted many seeds.

When seeds are planted in children,

Their lives begin to change indeed.

Yes, mother touched the future, she taught,

And hundreds of kids benefited from the seeds she planted, nourished, and grew.

We are unable to comprehend the kind of multiplication wrought,

When Jesus blesses lives that are turned over to Him anew.

Anyone can count the seeds in an apple,

But only God can count all the apples in one seed.

May He nourish and multiply the good in mother's life example,

And many grow and benefit by her good deeds.

Home is Where the Heart Is

Home is where the heart is,
The soul's bright guiding star.
Home is where real love is,
Where our own dear ones are.

Home means someone waiting
To give a welcome smile.
Home is worth contemplating,
It means peace, joy, rest, and everything worthwhile.

Home is made from love,
Warm as the golden light from a fire dancing on the floor.
Home is God's gift given from above,
It's simply a place where loved ones are, as we come through the door.

Home is a place we are yearning to be,
A place where work and play are properly in tune.
Home is where relationships flourish and people exist peaceably,
Where there's time for what's really important, and life is sheltered from ruin.

God, bless our home, and help us to love each other true;
To make our home the kind of place where everything we do
Is filled with love and kindness, a dwelling place for Thee,
And help us, God, each moment, to live most helpfully.

A Commuting Marriage

For Maggie ...

Driving across the high desert prairie's of Oregon
Thinking about my lonely life,
Separated in body, but not spirit from my home,
And commuting over 300 miles round trip on weekends to be with my wife.

The local economy has gone down hill
Leaving us in this terrible plight,
Causing my wife to move away to work and help pay the bills
By working long into the night.

I've had no pay raise since '97
Much to my chagrin,
And pray often for a pay increase to heaven,
So my wife and I can get back together again.

    Roll Toyota truck roll, across the prairie highways,
    Bringing us back together again.
    This constant separation during the weekdays,
    Makes my heart ache and grow fonder of you on the weekend.

I've learned to live for the weekend,
A commuting marriage has become my way of life.
I long to be with my best friend,
My lover, companion and wife.

I yearn for her sweet caress and the touch of her soft skin against my heart,

To see her ruby lips and the smile upon her face,

That lets me know she loves me still even though we've been apart,

Reminding me that commuting marriages are tough, but no disgrace.

When we finally see each other on the weekends we embrace,

As friends and lovers often do,

It's as lonely during the week for her as I, and it shows upon her face,

I kiss her cheek and wipe away her tears and remind her our love is solid and true.

Roll Toyota truck roll, across the prairie highways,

Bringing us back together again.

This constant separation during the weekdays,

Makes my heart ache and grow fonder of you on the weekend.

SOUL MATES

Two hearts soaring with love;

Bathed in the warm light of a crackling fire.

The young lovers need no words to express their innermost feelings that fit together like a glove.

Today they were married in the tradition of their people in Native American attire.

They are soul mates;

And as they join together through life and develop a strong bond,

Their love will only grow stronger following the path the sacred eagle makes,

Which soars ever higher on outstretched wings beyond.

CHAMP

Champ is my great little orange and white bundle of hunting energy.

He is a champion Brittany Spaniel pup with a superbly keen nose.

Champ likes to hunt at close range, point and retrieve.

He has great hunting desire, bird-finding ability, an appealing disposition, and as a pet, likes to be close.

Champ is still learning his basic commands and obedience training,

He responds to a whistle and hand signals.

He can sit and stay, but he still needs to learn come, whoa, heel, kennel, no, down, fetch, and retrieving.

And most of the time, as a five-month-old pup, he just likes to jump, run, and wiggle.

Champ pointed his first covey of chukars at three months old.

He is not timid, gun shy or a dog that will yield.

Champ is an alpha male with a wagging tail, enthusiasm, and a response that is bold.

He's still learning direction, range, and control in the field.

This gun dog of mine is an upland game bird hunter's delight.

And this weekend will be his first real hunting test.

I am sure Champ will hunt with all his skill and might,

And we may even limit out, proving he is one of the best.

(P.S. We did limit out!)

SCOOTER

Scooter is my black and burnt-orange colored male Chihuahua dog.

I rescued him from the Salem, Oregon pound for forty dollars in 1994.

During the day he sleeps like a log,

And he got his name because he wipes his butt by "scooting" across the carpeted floor.

Scooter looks like a small pot bellied miniature pig.

He's fat and he eats just about anything that I do.

When I come home, he twirls around and dances a jig,

And goes outside to take a "pee" and a "poo"!

Scooter has been given many names over the years.

He answers to these: Little Dog, Scruffy Little Mutt, Bat Ears, and Short Crotch.

My favorite name for him is Short Crotch, but I don't use it much in polite society around my peers.

Scooter is one of my best friends, and when he starts barking and playing, I just like to watch.

He barks and dances from side to side;

And he likes to bait me into playing a game of hide and seek.

But his favorite pastime by far is begging scraps from the table, I must confide.

Scooter whines, nuzzles, touches me with his paw and continues to beg by acting meek.

Most of all, Scooter is my constant companion when I am writing, composing poems, or all alone.

He welcomes me home when I return from a hard day's work at school.

And he jumps up on my lap when I sit in my favorite green leather chair and watch T.V., sleep, snore and groan.

In the end, I'd say that dogs are man's best friend as a general rule.

HAVE YOU SEEN MY GENUINE OLD TIMER WEATHER ROCK?

Have you seen my genuine old-timer weather rock?
I consult it daily, at the same time on my clock.

You simply tie it on a string,

    and hang it from a beam,

    outside on your front porch

and observe the following, even if by torch:

- If the rock is wet, it is raining.
- If the rock is white, it is snowing.
- If the rock is swinging, it is windy.
- If the rock is hard to see, it is foggy.
- If the rock is casting a shadow, it is sunny.
- If the rock is cold to the touch, it is cold out.
- If the rock is warm to the touch, it is warm out.
- If the rock is gone, you've been ripped off!

Old timer is never wrong!

So, purchase one of my genuine old-timer weather rock post cards at www. tlawinc.vpweb.com and join the throng.

Have You Seen My Genuine Oregon Rocky Mountain Elk Barometer?

Dedicated to elk hunters the world over ...

Have you seen my genuine Oregon Rocky Mountain Elk barometer?

You simply find an Oregon Rocky Mountain Elk, observe it, and monitor:

- When it's tail is dry, it is fair outside.
- When it's tail is wet, it is raining.
- When it's tail swings, it is windy.
- If it's tail is white, it is snowing.
- If it's tail is frozen, it is cold.
- If it's tail casts a shadow, it is sunny.
- If it's tail is invisible to the naked eye, it is foggy.
- If the elk falls over, you are having an earthquake or it got shot by another hunter!

Old timer is never wrong!

So, purchase one of My Genuine Oregon Rocky Mountain Elk Barometer Post Cards at www.tlawinc.vpweb.com and join the throng!

TIME

Time is like an athlete,

    Competing in the long-jump.

       It goes flying by,

          But doesn't seem to last.

             By the time it's here,

               It's past!

MY E-BAY EXPERIENCE

Wow, what a humorous experience I had the other day,
I signed up to bid as timadsrocks on e-Bay.

I needed a cornet or trumpet and started bidding on everything in sight.
Nobody bothered telling me you could make a list and just watch it throughout the day and night.

I bid on 15 or 20 horns at once figuring that I'd be outbid in the last minute.
As of today, I have won six horns and am still leading in five more auctions, and I am trying to see the humor in it.

It hasn't cost me an arm and a leg yet,
And it will be a learning experience I won't soon forget.

I may eat a little less as the month wears on,
To help defray the expense of just bidding on and on.

But, I'll either sell the extra horns back on e-Bay,
Or donate them to my local school and deduct them on tax day.

Either way, it's been rather fun I have to say,
Bidding on my e-Bay!

It's the Principal of the Hole Thing

Dedicated to those who stopped and pulled me out of the ditch.

I left Mary M. Knight School after a football game at about 4:00 p.m. o'clock;

And drove back down a road not far from the store at Matlock.

I was hunting black tail deer and trying to find the road behind the school in hot pursuit of a wily buck;

All the while driving my Toyota Sequoia 4-wheel that drives like a pick-up truck.

Earlier that afternoon I had been given careful directions and facts,

But apparently my ears were plugged with wax.

Because I ended up on the wrong road, not far from the main highway,

Stuck and high-centered with my wheels going every which way.

I couldn't even get my door open and get out of the truck,

There was absolutely no question, the High School Principal of MMK was stuck.

So I honked my horn at every vehicle that passed by

And smiled in hopes that someone would stop and give me some help by and by.

Help arrived shortly and they went for a chain to pull me out of a five foot hole with a tow;

But as fate would have it a crowd with cameras gathered wouldn't you know.

So I thought I'd write this poem to commemorate this Matlock hunting adventure and humorous fling,

Because, as we all know, it will probably end up on the store brag board under the title, "It's the Principal of the Hole Thing."

Thanks to you all who stopped that Saturday and rendered roadside assistance without fear,

Now just point me in the direction of that danged black tail buck deer.

Technology For Country Folk Who Spend Time In The Great Outdoors

We "Country Folk" have finally begun to get and use this new fangled technology.

One of the first steps has been to learn the terminology.

For example:

- Log On means makin' the stove hotter.
- Log Off means coolin 'er down.
- Monitor means keepin' an eye on 'er.
- Download means gitten the farwood off'n the truck.
- Megahertz means when you have an axe in your hand and yer not keerful gitten the farwood.
- Floppy Disk means whutcha git in your lower back from tryin ta tote too much farwood.
- Ram means that thar thing what splits farwood.
- Hard Drive means gitten your pickup home through two foot of snow in the winter time.
- Windows means whut ta shut when it's cold outside.
- Screen means whut ta shut when its black fly and mosquito season.
- Byte means whut dem dang flys and mosquitoes do.
- Chip means munchies fer the TV.
- Micro Soft Word means little soft words.
- Housing means duh thing datch yer livin' in.
- Software means under wear dat feels soft to the touch.
- Hardware means whut yer goin' to the hardware store to buy.
- Dell means a brand of pickle yer fond of puttin' on your sandwich.
- IBM means the sign that you give when you raise yer hand and tell the teacher you gotta go number two in the local schoolhouse.
- Mouse Balls means that if yer pet mouse fails to operate properly or should he perform erratically, he may need a ball replacement. Because of da delicate nature of this procedure, replacement of mouse balls should only be attempted by properly trained personnel.

- Pointer means whut yer huntin' dog duz with the quail in yer backyard.
- Power Points means whut yer mechanic is usin' when he's tunin' up yer pickup truck.
- Internet means that thar thing fisherman used to sein for minnows to catch bass and crappies.

The above samples are by now undoubtedly ample.

So, folks, if it's a moral to this story about technology you seek,

When things break down, call your logical, analytical, technology geek!

Themes About Retirement, Achieving Dreams
and Goals, Striving for Success in Life

RETIRE TO SOMETHING, NOT FROM SOMETHING

As my father used to say until my ears would ring;
When it comes time to retire, retire to not from something.

And I have found that to be sage advice and a statement full of wisdom.
My time has finally come to retire to something and not from.

In April of 2010, I retired into a life of hunting, fishing, golfing, reading, writing, real estate investing, internet franchising, ministering and other kinds of recreation,
From the pressure packed fields of education and school administration.

I plan to spend more time with family and friends as my retirement unfolds;
And continue to work on accomplishing my newly set life goals.

I keep these goals and dreams on a list complete with pictures above my desk,
And work towards them daily as if on a quest.

I plan to be active in retirement and continue to strive for success,
And leave behind all the former job pressures and stress.

Life is a journey, not a destination it would seem;
And to me, success is the progressive realization of a worthwhile goal or dream.

But in retirement I plan to simplify my life, while continuing to believe in my dreams,

And to see more with my heart to know what love really means.

ON FREEDOM'S WING

In 1782, the United States adopted as its emblem, the majestic, bald eagle with outspread wings, a shield upon its breast and holding an olive branch and sheaf of arrows in its talon.

The eagle has long stood, since Roman times, as a symbol of leadership, power, and progress, and it is a bird of superb strength, keenness of sight and possesses marvelous powers of flight.

So as the eagle soars high on freedom's wing, let your vision soar and lead you to greater heights of achievement, rallying you on.

And, as Americans, bring clear and purposeful thought to bear on your problems, and be strong and fearless in spirit and action and ever enjoy freedom's might.

For America's strength and beliefs have made this country home to people seeking freedom's ring.

We have no boundaries and no strings to bind us or keep us from our goals.

Like the bald eagle, we can soar to great heights, weather any storm, and achieve our dreams by riding on freedom's wing.

And, as individual Americans, we have learned to value freedom, the companionship, and the joy of being with others in beautiful surroundings and pursuing what life holds.

Home Of The Free, Because Of The Brave

America——Home of the free, because of the brave.

Many of our heroes died for you and me, so we wouldn't be slaves.

Listen! Can't you hear them calling through centuries of sacrifice, toil, and sleep;

From the heights of foreign mountain tops, they're calling, and from their lost ships sunk in oceans deep.

Can't you hear our fallen veterans calling from their distant battlefields and graves;

Saying, rise up against tierny, oppression, and terrorism, and keep America the land of the free and the home of the brave.

Their voices are saying, "rise up, don't allow our supreme sacrifice to be in vain,

And through all of our deaths and pain;

Remember that it's your right, legacy, duty and responsibility to preserve and save,

America as the home of the free, because of the brave."

On Freedom's Frontline

Dedicated to Sgt. Jason Adsit, my son, who served in Afghanistan and received the bronze star.

Today, men and women across the U.S. are stepping forward to protect freedom and their fellow Americans.

They're on freedom's front lines.

But freedom isn't as free as it sounds.

It requires vigilance at all times.

Freedom isn't free,

People are dying for you and me,

On freedom's frontlines.

Most serve so they can answer the Nations call, whenever, wherever, and for as long as they are needed.

Daily they preserve life, liberty and are in the pursuit of all who threaten it.

Through their valor, toil, sacrifice and courage, they have succeeded,

In protecting American's most valued asset.

Freedom isn't free,

People are dying for you and me,

On freedom's frontlines.

The Dead Live On

Dedicated to America's Veterans ...

This year we stop to breathe a prayer,

For the men and women who have died over there;

We see the breathless bodies, the life is gone,

But the lips they murmur, "the dead live on".

Pass the word along, "the dead live on."

They have not died in vane, who left us with a smile,

For we all our only here on earth a little while.

We remember before Thee those who in time of peace were called to war;

Those who forsook all to answer the call: soldiers, sailors, airmen, chaplains, nurses, doctors, engineers, laborers—all who went forth and returned no more.

Pass the word along, "the dead live on."

Lift up the light of Thy countenance upon all who suffered for us, especially now those who are broken in body, or clouded in mind, or hurt in soul.

May our gratitude never fail or our sympathetic help never waiver; help us to bear another's burdens and so fulfill Christ's law of old.

Pass the word along, "the dead live on."

Father of mercies, hear us as we pray for these fallen heroes, and deliver our souls and theirs, and our nation from whatever would shame their memory; and make us worthier of their bloodshed.

Bring good from evil, turn wrath to praise; quench pride and anger, and teach us to do justly, to love mercy, and to walk humbly before thee, our God of the living, and not the dead.

Pass the word along, "the dead live on."

And now, O God, may thy benediction of peace, forgiveness, and mercy; fall upon this sacred place, as we leave here may we carry with us new resolves to be better Americans;

Better men and women, so that our lives will give honor to those whose memories we cherish; and most of all may we resolve to so live and die that our freedoms will be passed on to our children and friends.

Pass the word along, "the dead live on, the dead live on, the dead live on!"

Recurring Themes About Hunting,
Fishing, Hiking, and Camping

IMPRESSIONS OF AN EARLY SEASON ARCHERY HUNT

Camping in wild lands carrying you back to wilder days,
Enjoying the thrill of the early season elk hunt;
Resorting to using old fashioned grunts, chirps, and bugling ways,
And the excitement of calling in bulls in the rut.

Wary bulls sneaking through the lodge poles,
Antlers swaying and flung back;
Dodging pursuing hunters with compound bows,
Who are after their trophy sized rack.

A hunter's moon low in the western sky,
The tangy smell of sage in the cool morning air,
Hearing a coyote's haunting cry,
Such are the impressions that define the open day of archery season this year.

INTO THE MIDDLE FORK OF THE JOHN DAY

Climb aboard one of our mountain horses, join us, and get away,

Where canyons rarely echo a rifle shot,

And ridges give you postcard views of more elk habitat than you can hunt in a day,

And sleep in a big white wall tent far from the trailhead and office coffeepot.

We hunt the old fashioned way, mainly from horseback,

You'll get food so good you'll think you're at grandma's shack,

A hot shower and sound sleep because each night it's pitch black,

And a guaranteed chance at a big bull and memories that won't fade, but call you back.

You won't be hunting country that has been pressured much by other hunters,

Instead we'll probe farther into the wilderness gates,

So come and join us our hunting sisters and brothers,

And we'll give you the best trip of your life to date.

Into the Middle Fork of the John Day at Tent Cliff Outfitters Camp

I Like Men Who Hunt

I like men who hunt! Men who seek the challenge and the comfort of the forests, the rivers, the streams, the meadows, the thickets, the bogs, and the mountains.

Men—who laughing say, "When my time comes to go, let it be with an elk or deer within my rifle sights and range, and on the other end me just pulling the trigger." Let it be like that dear Lord, when the final call comes.

Let me be there—on some mountain game trail, with loved ones or friends… happy, hoping for a royal bull, or a "hooter" buck…let me be showing my faith…that I will shoot a trophy sized animal before the day is done…there… call me home…suddenly…free me from my physical limitations.

And when I arrive in my heavenly home…just one request dear Lord, for all who have gone before me…those good friends of mine who love to hunt… let them be there to welcome me…And Lord, give me a job, make me keeper of the forests, the rivers, the streams, the meadows, the thickets, the bogs, and the mountains filled with trophy elk and deer…for that will be Heaven to me.

I Like Men Who Hunt

In Search of Solitude and Trout

Dedicated to Glyn Adsit, Francis Ives, Gene and Bill Terway who were fishing companions over the years.

In search of solitude and trout,

That's what scouting, hiking in, camping, and fishing the wilderness lakes is all about.

The experience and solitude of fishing Oregon's wilderness lakes more than makes up for the lack of inches in fish.

Most fish are just big enough to fit into the pan, and will look, and taste good next to some onions, potatoes and lemon slices in a dish.

Every summer in my youth, I used to take a few weekends and get away from the hustle and bustle of the local fishing scene.

There is also something about a brook trout dinner that just reminds me of summertime outings and outdoor cuisine.

So, for the intrepid angler willing to swap boat or car for hiking boots and pack,

There is a bounty of fishing opportunity available in Oregon's wilderness outback.

The Spike and the Royal Bull

Dedicated to Don House, disabled veteran, hunting companion and friend ...

It was day five of the elk hunt and I left Sags Motel before first light at about 5:00 o'clock.

I drove my Toyota Tundra pickup truck past the Fireside Lodge, Austin House, Clear Creek, Grant County Road 20, and up a creek named Murdock.

> Upon arriving at our elk camp in Grandma's Saddle below Buck Mountain, Don and I had coffee in our outfitters tent, and we discussed the wind's direction and how he would hunt the hollows hard.

> My role during the morning's hunt was to drive down to take a stand looking over a clearing by the old wrought iron cattle guard.

After watching and waiting for about two hours, I finally saw the herd running off the Ponderosa covered mountain bank, churning up the ground into mulch.

Don and I continued to pursue these wily elk across the gravel road, past the old corral and watering trough into a dry gully known as Hunt Gulch.

> Then, we finally caught up with the herd and sighted a spike and Royal 7-point bull just as the elk bailed over a steep ridge into a creek named Windlass.

> Don went down one draw and I went down another, still in pursuit of the bulls which by now had slowed down to rest and eat some grass.

We converged on them at the bottom of a canyon, and we each took a shot at about the same time. The bulls ran out of sight to the West where they climbed a knoll and went straight up.

In fast pursuit now, we tracked their blood trails and found them later that day just before noon, where the spike and Royal bull fell dead on a wooded hill in a creek called Tincup.

> We dressed both bulls out and drug them to an old abandoned Sumpter Railroad bed where we were able to drive in, load them, and bring them out whole.

> Once back in our camp, we used pulleys and rope to string both bulls up on an often-used Jack Pine meat pole.

And that ends the saga of our elk hunt that November day outside Prairie City, Oregon where we were successful in shooting the spike and Royal 7-point bull.

We'll be back, though, to hunt again another year, but for now our freezers at home are full.

OPENING DAY CHUKAR HUNT

Sitin home relaxing now while watchin Gunsmoke,
After a day of Chukar huntin on a rim rock slope.

The dog and I got up about six and took the Toyota truck for a drive,
And we ended up traveling towards Riverside.

We stopped at a spring on the side of a hill,
And as the sun came over an eastern slope, I called in our first Chukars with
a special shrill.

A covey of about twenty birds answered back the series of calls,
And as they flew I knocked down two with my double barrel twelve gauge
containing shells filled with #6 steal shot balls.

Then all at once, the whole hillside of rock, cheat grass and sage exploded,
And more Chukars flew in every direction before I could get reloaded.

So the dog and I hunted this promising area for the rest of the day,
Jumping small groups of birds until getting a limit of eight along the way.

ONE OF LIFE'S SPECIAL MOMENTS
BETWEEN FATHER AND SON

Dedicated to Justin …

It was on the second day of the High Cascade deer hunt with my son Justin,

And we were up before daylight, had breakfast, and traveled to Jack Pine road.

Around noon we headed up a very steep, boulder and Juniper branch filled four-wheel drive goat-trail trying to keep the pickup paint from being scratched and windows from bustin;

And we eventually came to road's end by the backside base of Hoo Doo's rocky geode.

We gazed to the south at Mount Washington and Big Lake far below,

And immediately knew this was one of life's special moments between father and son.

Though it was high noon and the light was directly overhead providing no shadow,

I took a picture for posterity's sake and pasting in the hunting and fishing scrapbook for looking at together during future times to come.

*One of Life's Special Moments Between Father and Son. We gazed
to the South at Mount Washington and Big Lake Far Below*

This will always be remembered as our special time and place,

Where life's ambitions, goals, and dreams were discussed,

As we just starred at nature's beauty and gazed off into the distant space;

And filled our hearts, souls and minds with God's great outdoors so wondrous
to behold, proclaiming that returning there someday will be a must.

Our quality time together that fall afternoon,

Became more of a priority than killing a "Hooter Bench Buck."

We just enjoyed each other's company knowing we had to part too
soon,

But vowed to get back together for some "quantity family time" during
the upcoming elk hunt where we will tent camp, beat the brush again
together, and go four-wheeling in my Toyota pickup truck.

Like Looking for a Needle in a Haystack

Finding a spike elk in Oregon's Desolation Unit outback,
Is like looking for a needle in an Eastern Oregon cattle ranchers haystack.

You know that there is a spike out there somewhere,
But shooting one is like trying to catch the wind in the air.

Spike elk seem to be rather illusive,
And they are a sought after trophy that is very exclusive.

They stay in hiding during hunting season,
And appear in odd places and times almost without reason.

I guess that's why I enjoy hunting them, for the shear challenge I aspire;
Even though other's comments about my success rate leave a lot to be desired.

Spike hunting has become for me like a quest,
And I prefer not to follow the road like the rest.

Though I could draw other unit tags,
Instead, I will keep hunting spike elk until this "trophy" is in the bag.

LIVE THE WILD

Elk camp was set up on Buck Mountain above the middle fork of the John Day River by mid morning,

A Nor'Wester was blowing in and it was sleeting and snowing.

The Quik Kamp outfitters wall tent went up in about an hour, complete with frame, flaps, stove, tie-downs and an awning.

And, after gathering and cutting Tamarack for firewood and splitting it, a warm and crackling fire was started with embers glowing.

Loyal friends, getting together in secret spaces,

Named and known only by the hunters who were there.

Grandma's Saddle, the Bull Pen, Drop-a-Load-Road, The Airport, Vinegar, Caribou, Little Boulder, Murdock, Hunt Gulch, Tincup, Windless, and other places…

Those are the best spots, which often come with a story told with a great deal of flare.

Let every aspect of hunting bring excitement to your life.

Woods living, trees living, nature living with nature, live the wild.

Trigger your passion, release your strife.

Keep your senses well honed and filed.

Feel the wind on your face and hear, drifting down from way back in some hanging basin, that high, wild sound.

There is no way you can put a price on the experience of watching or hearing a royal bull split the dawn with a bugle so shrill.

Capture the thrill of the hunt, adventures abound.

Demonstrate courage, strength, grit, and an iron will.

It's out there.

Go get it.

Live the wild, and smell the fresh air.

Get out, exercise, and hunt a bit.

While elk hunting, you'll see cows which define grace and remind us where every bull comes from.

But there's no point denying the power and allure of a bull's horns.

And calves are bright-spotted promises of hunts to come,

So venture into the wild in fall with its colors adorned.

On Any Given Sunday During Hunting Season

On any given Sunday, some guys focus on point spreads.

For me, after church, it's all about the points on the rack.

A day of watching hulking gladiators chase the pig skin in their Lycra threads,

Or, a day hunting elk and packing a bull from the outback.

It's no contest, which one I would choose.

Give me the hair-raising sound of a big bull's bugle rising up from the bottom of a backcountry canyon.

The cold, clear nights spent on the side of a mountain, these are the things I dream of when I snooze.

And I have continued this hunting legacy through fifty years with reckless abandon.

I'll be up there this fall, perhaps I'll meet you there.

The coming elk season guarantees at least a few surprises.

Steep climbs, sore muscles, blistered feet, but I am tougher than Mother Nature's fare.

When my adrenaline is pumping, years of experience and hunting simplicity usually brings home the back strap prize.

Hunting simplicity like a steady gun and steady nerves.

And using a shooting stick, designed to steady a firearm on any terrain.

As first light creeps over the horizon on opening morning, I anticipate belly crawling across the edge of a favorite meadow toward the grazing elk herds.

And shooting a seven point Rocky Mountain bull elk with a dark coated mane.

IT'S YOUR MOMENT OF TRUTH

Good friends, campfires, and stories of past adventures are on hold for later this evening, it's opening day, and you're alone.

A frigid dawn turns into day and you're perched motionless in a tree stand overlooking the fresh elk sign located last night by the wallow and tree with pine cones.

There! At the edge of the meadow slough, the dark brown and buckskin form slinks along the edge with uncanny silence and flare.

Your vitals go into red alert as you try to calm your heart beat with forced, steady breaths released slowly into the air.

His non-typical rack, which will score over 400 Boone and Crockett points, dips behind brush as you silently rise and begin to take careful aim through your Leupold scope.

The bull stares transfixed at your strange apparition in the tree, so tense you thought you could see his legs shaking in the grass, but the wind is in your favor, and you have on a camouflage coat.

He grunts quietly, ignores you, then gently bobs his head up and down as if feeding.

It's your moment of truth and the sweat on your brow begins beading.

Your mind processes an astounding amount of information in a few short-moments, especially when life and death hang in the balance with one trigger pull.

And, as you squeeze the trigger hitting the elk in a vital spot, you take satisfaction knowing that this time you won the extreme close-encounter game of stealth between man and the elusive seven point bull.

Just "Gittin" Out Amongst "Em"

(Dedicated to Chris Wood, Loren Bebb, Buell Gonzales, Chuck Steeves, Larry Conaway, Dwane Thompson, and Dave Doman … friends who love to get out amongst em!)

It's the thrill of first catching sight of that trophy elk during opening day;

The sound of chipmunks and squirrels making noise in the Ponderosa Pine forests at play.

It's the smell of a smoky campfire drifting up through the beautiful aspen in the morning sun;

And all the stories passed down from grandfather and father to daughter or son.

It's preserving your memories on the written page in a journal, scrapbook and on film just for fun;

To be enjoyed by friends, family, and generations to come.

It's just "gittin out amongst 'em" in the wilderness, enjoying beauty and nature;

And the opportunity to freely pursue the wily creature.

It's where it all starts, where children first grasp the importance of preserving our cherished outdoor tradition;

Where sportsmen and their friends and families experience first-hand the majesty and grandeur of the great outdoors and catch the vision.

It's the lessons learned here that can help change a concerned sportsmen's world for the better;

And provide an unforgettable experience, a walk on the wild side with hope for a future and legacy of big-game hunting unfettered.

No Trophy As Rewarding As the Hunt Itself

I have enjoyed hunting in the wide-open spaces of the Western United States for over fifty years.

Open terrain, from rim rock to sage, from treetop canopies to open rangeland.

I've been privileged to hunt for many species including elk, deer, varmints, turkey, chukar partridge, quail, grouse, pronghorn antelope, big horn sheep, and bears.

Each wild game species has turned these wide-open spaces into hiding places so grand.

Now, it's time to reflect and commemorate the hunt and all its splendor and wander.

I've always been an ethical hunter who strives with all my might to always be safe, be lawful, kill cleanly with one shot, fully utilize the animal harvested, and practice fair chase.

The hunter's path has been long, interesting, and rewarding, and I have learned through the years to never stop learning, and to pass my knowledge and wisdom on to family friends, and others.

And, I have enjoyed no trophy as rewarding as the hunt itself with all of its' simplicity and grace.

No two hunts have been the same; they have all been unique.

But, by far, the thrill of first catching sight of that trophy elk, the smell of a smoky campfire drifting up through the aspen or ponderosa, all the stories passed down from grandfather and father to son or daughter, that has been the best.

Looking for elk year after year has been like looking for love; since options can vanish fast and looking in the wrong places can cost you the ultimate prize even when you are at your peak.

I continue to carry on the hunting tradition in the great outdoors, it's easier than ever to give back to the sport I love and that has overtime stood the test.

Going Afield

When the love is flowing in a family, life is honey sweet.

Add elk hunting and wild country, and the feeling is hard to beat.

Family ties, stories about old hunters, young hunters, the long unbroken stream of generations passing through;

Loving, sharing, taking life, giving life back, exploring, encountering, experiencing, it's what we do.

Going afield, where wildlife is still wild, you want it never to end;

So you pass it on, taking time to bond with family and friends.

Sitting around the campfire cooking, eating, talking, and whittling, the night before, knowing the hunt is at hand;

You realize that you truly are a steward of the elk and the land.

It's morning now, you are far from base camp;

The sleet is falling fast, the temperature is falling even faster, and the air is damp.

You're on an elk stand watching and waiting, the weather conditions take a turn for the worst;

Is it time to head back to camp or is it time, to push your hunting and yourself to the extreme first?

The hunt—will you push it to its limits or will it push you to discover yours in the end?

This is a question often asked and pondered by myself and my hunting friends.

Nothing is better than hunting for my family, friends, and me,

The feeling is often beyond words, for at the end of the day there is no trophy as rewarding as the hunt itself you see.

Going the distance, just being out amongst them;

At the end of the day, it's not just what you killed, but how you hunted 'em.

By just being in God's great outdoors, my family and I have been blessed;

Knowing, as John Muir once said, "that the clearest way into the Universe is through the forest wilderness."

A SMALL CABIN IS BEAUTIFUL

I will rise up and go now to Bend,

And a small cabin there of logs, cedar siding, and stones made:

Several fenced garden rows will I have there, humming bird feeders, and a bird bath for my fine feathered friends,

And live alone in the valley, surrounded by Ponderosa and Juniper forests, the Cascade Mountains, red and grey lava rock, and green, grassy meadow glade.

Set in the city like a hidden jewel,

On a clear day, the cabin has an awe inspiring ten (10) snow capped peaks mountain view.

And gazing upon this wondrous sight causes inner renewal,

One never gets tired of picturesque sunrises and sunsets, and the mountains constantly changing shades and colorful hues.

And I shall have some peace and tranquility there, for peace comes descending slow.

Dropping from the foggy veils of the mountain morning mist to where the bird sings.

There midnight's sparkling from the bright, twinkling stars above, and noon a purple, rosy glow,

And evening full of the eagle's wings.

I will rise up and go now, for always night and day,

I hear crystal clear creek water running with low sounds by the cabin door;

While I stand on the deck, or on the pavement gray,

I hear it in my very heart and soul's core.

My cabin is a place of personal freedom, a retreat;

It's a place for quiet contemplation, to think great thoughts and to simplify one's life.

Those who are invited there come to hunt, fish, write, pursue a favorite hobby, visit, or just rest and take a load off their mind and feet.

The cabin is a place to leave the hustle and bustle of the world behind with all its daily strife.

My small cabin is beautiful and serene,

A place to go and one's spirit renew;

A place to be creative, set goals and dream,

And invite my closest new and old friends and family, just a few.

THE GOOD LIFE

It's all part of the pleasure of living in and dreaming of elk country.

The smell of boots and saddles, wet wool and wood smoke,

Horses and canvas, sagebrush and pine trees.

And grand mountain vistas in places remote.

The Good Life is about wild freedom and no fear,

The comforts of good food and of camp,

The security and pleasure of good friends and good gear,

And dryness and shelter from the damp.

It's all part of the Good Life,

As our fellow hunter-conservationists before and since have envisioned it and lived it.

We must work to ensure outdoor adventure in elk country with all our might,

And we owe it to ourselves to get out there and enjoy it, every bit.

Outdoor adventures in elk country must be cherished, preserved and made available for generations to come.

Take some new folks with you this fall.

Invite a friend outdoors with you to share the good life some,

And share the hunt with them, prepare them, teach them, equip them, and then turn them loose to pass it on to others who will also share the wildlife heritage call.

SANCTUARY AT THE EDGE OF THE CITY

Walking up the road to the east of my cabin brings you to the edge of Bend.

After a short while, you come to a well worn trail used for hiking or off road mountain biking.

The trail winds around for several miles over public lands owned by the BLM.

It is a great place to come for exercise and the terrain is quite striking.

At the ground level is the sandy volcanic ash and loam found on the Central Oregon high desert.

The land is covered by gray lava rock outcroppings and small potholes sink downward while small hills and mounds rise up into the air.

Ancient juniper trees, cheat grass, and sage provide ground cover and help hold the desert earth.

Golden throated doves and quail chirp, coo, sing, fly, nest, and live there.

The trail area also provides a place for coyote and mule deer to walk, run, and live in.

And my neighbors and I sometimes walk our dogs there, both getting exercise and fresh air.

The trail provides a sanctuary at the edge of the city away from the traffic noise and din.

It' a tranquil place for me to reflect, think, and mediate found only a short walk from my log cabin home located near there.

Where Earth and Heaven Meet

From where I write

I take great delight

In looking past our cabin door

To where eagles soar.

In the distance, out across a gently rippling stream

I see rolling foothills leading to snow capped peaks bathed in misty morning fog and steam.

These hills and mountains seem to keep communion with the sky,

And I think of many other horizons where earth and heaven meet the eye.

Besides that distant union of earth and sky just beyond my cabin door,

There are countless other horizons where Ponderosa and Jack Pine forests rise with a constant urgency toward the sun and stars galore.

Where the jagged mountains point volcanic fingers at heaven's grace,

And where the timeless lakes and waterfalls and eternal sky embrace.

Nature abounds with meeting places welling up where heaven meets land,

But the most impressive horizon I know of is a creature called "man."

It is here, in man, where earth and heaven meet without facade.

Man is the meeting place of the dust of the ground and the breath of God.

Man, like a horizon, is where earth and heaven meet,

Where the lowest and the highest come together like a seamless pleat.

Man is a horizon where earth and heaven meet within,

But great manhood and womanhood is where heaven and earth meet, and Heaven wins.

Beautiful Small Custom Log Cabin

Additional Books by the Author, Projects in the Works and Contact Information

In addition to this collection of poetry, Tim L. Adsit has written several books that have been published nationally by Rowman and Littlefield Education, Lanham, Maryland. His books include:

- *Practical Ideas for Cutting Costs and Ways to Generate Alternative Revenue Sources,* 2005;
- *Cutting Costs and Generating Revenues in Education,* Second Edition, December 2010;
- *Surviving Economic, Social, and Environmental Distress—Small Schools, Education, and the Importance of Community,* May 2011 (in production), which focuses on the leadership role of small schools in helping to revitalize small school and community development and long-term improvement.

Upcoming projects by Tim Adsit in the final stages of writing, editing, and design that will be published in the near future include:

- *Fisher's of Men,* the biography of Reverend Glyn and Jean Adsit's lives and ministry;
- *Driven*— to Compete, Serve, Lead, and Succeed, An American Story, the autobiography of Tim Adsit;
- *Leadership for Personal Strategic Planning,* focusing on aligning organizational, departmental, and personal strategic planning for goal accomplishment and success;
- *Seeds of Change: Beacons for the Coming of His Light,* an in depth historical, photo essay and book on Reverend Glyn and Jean Adsit's missionary service in Hofei, China from 1944-1948 featuring never before published photographs of Chiang Kai Shek and Madame Chiang Kai Shek, and 120 other narrated photos taken by Reverend Adsit while in the mission field;

- *Marketing Yourself: A Resource Guide for Educational Administrators,* which covers everything from A to Z in how to market yourself and get hired in the 21st Century;
- *Strategically Planning, Developing, and Implementing Permanent School Closure in School Organizations.* The title explains it all;
- *All We Know About Fishing and Fisherman,* which features a written introduction by Reverend B. Adsit written just before he died, and co-authored chapters by my biological children, Darcy, Jason, and Justin Adsit, and myself; and
- *You Know You Are Rural When, You Know You Are Urban When, and You Know You Are Urban When ... , a series of humorous gift and table top books with original illustrations and short quotes.*

Contact Information:

You may contact the author at: Tim L. Adsit, TLAW, Inc., 20730 Barton Crossing Way, Bend, Oregon 97701-7711, Phone: (541) 383-5119; E-Mail: timads@bendbroadband.com; Web address: www.tlawinc.vpweb.com